Croc at the Dentist

'Croc at the Dentist'
An original concept by Jenny Jinks
© Jenny Jinks 2022

Illustrated by Katarina Gasko

Published by MAVERICK ARTS PUBLISHING LTD
Studio 11, City Business Centre, 6 Brighton Road,
Horsham, West Sussex, RH13 5BB
© Maverick Arts Publishing Limited May 2022
+44 (0)1403 256941

A CIP catalogue record for this book is available at the British Library.

ISBN 978-1-84886-879-3

www.maverickbooks.co.uk

This book is rated as: Blue Band (Guided Reading)
It follows the requirements for Phase 4 phonics.
Most words are decodable, and any non-decodable words are familiar,
supported by the context and/or represented in the artwork.

Croc at the Dentist

By Jenny Jinks

Illustrated by Katarina Gasko

Croc had lots of big teeth.

He liked to flash them in a big grin.

Zak went to see Croc.

But Croc was in a grump.

"Will you come and play?" said Zak.

"No!" said Croc.

"No need to snap!" said Zak.

Ellis went to see Croc.

"Will you come for dinner?" said Ellis.

"No!" said Croc.

"No need to snap!" said Ellis.

"What is up with Croc?" said Zak.

"He just snaps and snaps!"

They all agreed. They had to help Croc.

They went back to see Croc.

"Boo hoo!" Croc said.

Snap! Snap! Snap!

"No need to snap," said Ellis.

"We can help," said Zak.

"It is my tooth," said Croc.

"Can you look?"

The animals did not get near Croc's teeth.

"You need a dentist," said Ellis.

"I will not see a dentist!" said Croc.

But Croc's tooth pain did not stop.

So Croc went to see Doctor Nash, the dentist.

Croc sat back in the chair.

"Oh dear," said Doctor Nash.

"It will have to come out."

"Not my tooth!" said Croc.

Doctor Nash tugged and tugged…

"It was a stick!" said Doctor Nash.

"A stick was stuck!"

"My tooth!" said Croc.

"I am not in pain!"

Croc felt lots better.

He flashed his big teeth.

Snap! Snap! Snap!

Croc was happy.

Quiz

1. Croc has lots of big…
a) eyes
b) teeth
c) feet

2. What put Croc in a grump?
a) His tooth
b) The dentist
c) His friends

3. Who did Croc need to see?
a) A friend
b) A dentist
c) A wizard

4. What was the dentist's name?
a) Doctor Nash
b) Doctor Wash
c) Doctor Mash

5. What was stuck in Croc's teeth?
a) A leaf
b) A seed
c) A stick

Book Bands for Guided Reading

The Institute of Education book banding system is a scale of colours that reflects the various levels of reading difficulty. The bands are assigned by taking into account the content, the language style, the layout and phonics. Word, phrase and sentence level work is also taken into consideration.

Maverick Early Readers are a bright, attractive range of books covering the pink to white bands. All of these books have been book banded for guided reading to the industry standard and edited by a leading educational consultant.

To view the whole Maverick Readers scheme, visit our website at www.maverickearlyreaders.com

Or scan the QR code above to view our scheme instantly!

Quiz Answers: 1b, 2a, 3b, 4a, 5c